Quick and Effective Mandarin Chinese Guide for Beginners

Tina .O Peters

All rights reserved. Copyright © 2023 Tina .O Peters

Funny helpful tips:

In the realm of possibilities, dream big, but act with intention and purpose.

Prioritize customer feedback; it's a goldmine for product/service improvement.

Quick and Effective Mandarin Chinese Guide for Beginners : Master Mandarin Chinese in Record Time with this Expertly Crafted Beginner's Guide

Life advices:

In the meadow of memories, cherish the moments that resonate with love and joy.

Practice regular check-ins; they ensure both partners are on the same page.

Introduction

This is a comprehensive language resource that guides newcomers on their journey to mastering Mandarin.

Starting with essential greetings, learners are introduced to fundamental conversational elements. Formalities, etiquette, and politeness are emphasized, helping students navigate Chinese culture effectively. Daily living aspects are explored, ensuring learners can communicate in everyday situations, such as introductions and discussing time.

One significant focus of the workbook is reading and writing, catering to a well-rounded language education. Reading exercises provide practical texts to enhance vocabulary and comprehension, while writing exercises guide learners through the complex world of Chinese characters, including stroke order.

Idioms, an integral part of Chinese language and culture, are also covered. Understanding these idiomatic expressions adds depth to language proficiency and cultural awareness. Throughout the workbook, learners engage in structured exercises, gradually building their skills in a progressive manner.

By the end of this workbook, learners will have acquired essential language skills and cultural insights to confidently communicate in Mandarin Chinese.

Contents

Chapter 1: Greetings 1
Chapter 2: Formalities 12
Chapter 3: Daily Living 30
Chapter 4: Reading and Writing 64
Reading Exercises 64
    Short Story 1 65
    Short Story 2 67
    Short Story 3 69
Writing Exercises 72
Idioms 76
    Idiom 1 76
    Idiom 2 79
    Idiom 3 81
    Idiom 4 84
    Idiom 5 87
    Idiom 6 89

Chapter 1: Greetings

One of the most common sets of phrases is "hello" and "thank you". Along with these are some common forms of initials and finals that should be constantly practiced. It is advised that you say these out loud in order to hear yourself and how you sound.

Hello

Context Specific Dialogues

Dialogue 1: Saying "Hello" to one other person.

Person A: Hello.
 你好。
 Nǐ hǎo.

Person B: Hello.
 你好。
 Nǐ hǎo.

Dialogue 2: Saying "Hello" to more than one person.

Person A: Hello.

你们好。

Nǐ men hǎo.

Persons B and C: Hello.

你好。

Nǐ hǎo.

Non-Context Specific Dialogue

Dialogue 3: Apologizing.

Person A: I'm sorry!

对不起!

Duì bù qǐ!

Person B: That's okay, it does not matter!

没事，没关系!

Méi shì, méi guān xì!

Initials and Finals

Initials and Finals that need to be studied:

Initials	Finals
b	i
p	u
m	ü
f	er
d	a
t	ia
n	ua
l	o

g	uo
k	e
h	ie
j	ue
q	ai
x	uai
	ei
	uei (ui)
	ao
	iao

Thank You

Context-Specific Dialogues

Dialogue 1: Saying "Thank you" to one other person.

Person A: Thank you!

    谢谢你!

        Xiè xiè nǐ!

Person B: Sure!

    不客气!

    Bù kè qì!

Dialogue 2: Saying "Thank you" to an elder (or a person that is older than you are).

Person A: Thank you!

    谢谢您!

     Xiè xiè nín!

Persons B and C: You are welcome!
   不客气!
   Bù kè qì!

Dialogue 3: Informally saying "Goodbye."

Person A: Goodbye!
   再见!
     Zài jiàn!

Person B: Bye!
   再见!
     Zài jiàn!

Initials and Finals

Initials and finals that need to be studied:

Initials	Finals
zh	ou
ch	iou (iu)
sh	an
r	ian
z	uan
c	üan
s	en
	in
	uen (un)
	ün
	ang
	iang

	uang
	eng
	ing
	ueng
	ong
	iong

New Words and Phrases

It is important that you are always adding to your vocabulary each and every time you study Mandarin. In this section, we are going to give you some fun new words to try out, as well as their pinyin and Chinese characters so that you can start to recognize them in sentences and conversations. Don't forget to practice writing them in the spaces provided.

- One

    一

    Yī

- Two

    二

    Èr

- Three

    三

    San

- Four

    四

    Sì

- Five

    五

    Wǔ

- Six

    六

Liù

- Seven

七

Qī

- Eight

八

Bā

- Nine

九

Jiǔ

- Ten

十

Shí

- Jacket

夹克

Jiákè

- Fish

鱼

Yú

- Ear

耳

Ěr

- Pen

笔

Bǐ

- Cat

猫

Māo

- Island

岛

Dǎo _____

- Flower

  花

  Huā _____

- Chicken

  鸡

  Jī _____

- Shoes

  鞋

  Xié _____

- Summer

  春

  Chūn _____

- Spring

  夏

  Xià _____

- Autumn

  秋

  Qiū _____

- Winter

  冬

  Dōng _____

- Clock

  时钟

  Shí zhōng _____

- Hand

  手

  Shǒu _____

- Bear

  熊 _____

　　　　Xióng　　　　_____
- Clouds
　　　　云
　　　　Yún　　　　　_____
- Stars
　　　　星星
　　　　Xīng xīng　_____
- Friend
　　　　朋友
　　　　Péng yǒu　　_____
- Apple
　　　　苹果
　　　　Píng guǒ　　 _____
- Bed
　　　　床
　　　　Chuáng　　　 _____
- Panda
　　　　熊猫
　　　　Xióng māo　　_____
- Watch
　　　　手表
　　　　Shǒu biǎo　　_____
- Ball
　　　　球
　　　　Qiú　　　　　_____
- Egg
　　　　蛋
　　　　Dàn　　　　　_____
- Hamburger
　　　　汉堡包　　　 _____

- Hàn bǎo bāo
- McDonalds
    麦当劳
    Mài dāng láo
- Adidas
    阿迪达斯
    Ā dí dá sī
- Nike
    耐克
    Nài kè
- David Beckham
    大卫 贝克汉姆
    Dà wèi bèi kè hàn mǔ
- Harry Potter
    哈利 波特
    Hā lì bō tè
- Class begins.
    上课
    Shàng kè
- Class is over.
    下课
    Xià kè
- Look at this.
    看这个
    Kàn zhè ge
- Read after me.
    随我念
    Suí wǒ niàn
- Read together.
    一起念

Yī qǐ niàn _____

- Any questions?

  有问题吗 _____

  Yǒu wèn tí ma? _____

Chapter 2: Formalities

It is customary to ask individuals a few questions when you first meet them. As someone who is still at the beginning phases of learning Mandarin, it is vital that you ask these questions at all encounters, not only so that you become comfortable with asking them, but also to hone your skills. These questions can feel rather intimidating the first time that they are asked, but they will become second-nature as soon as you start to interact with a wider variety of those who speak Mandarin.

Use what you have learned in the previous chapter to start stringing together the beginning of a conversation as you would typically do in English.

Names

Context Specific Dialogue

Dialogue 1: Asking someone for their name.

Person A: What is your name?

                    你的名字叫什么?
          Nǐ de míng zì jiào shén me?

Person B: My name is Xiao Ming.
我的名字叫小明。
Wǒ de míng zì jiào Xiao Míng.

Non-Context Specific Dialogues

Dialogue 2: Asking whether someone is a teacher or not.

Person A: Are you a teacher?
你是老师吗?
Nǐ shì lǎo shī ma?

Person B: No, I am not. I am a student.
不, 我不是. 我是学生。
Bù, wǒ bù shì, wǒ shì xué shēng.

Dialogue 3: Enquiring whether someone is Chinese.

Person A: Are you Chinese?
你是中国人吗?
Nǐ shì Zhōng Guó rén ma?

Person B: No, I am not. I am French.
不，我不是，我是法国人。
Bù, wǒ bù shì, wǒ shì Fà guó rén.

Practice Dialogues

It is important to avoid only translating from English to Mandarin. By doing this, you are teaching yourself to think in one direction, which will hinder the speed at which you make progress. What we want you to do here is to read the pinyin, and then write down what you think the Chinese characters are based on the pinyin, as well as the English translation. Once you have completed this, check your answers and refine your translations. You can then go ahead and answer the question in pinyin and Chinese characters to ensure you understand everything that has been taught thus far.

Dialogue 1:

Nǐ jiào shén me míng zi?

你 叫 什 么 名 字 ?

What is your name?

Answer:
_____
_____
_____
_____

_____

Dialogue 2:
Nǐ shì Zhōng Guó rén ma?
你是中国人吗?
Are you Chinese?

Answer:
_____
_____
_____
_____

_____

Dialogue 3:
Nǐ shì Měi guó rén ma?
你是美国人吗?
Are you American?

Answer:
_____
_____
_____
_____

_____

Dialogue 4:
Nǐ shì lǎo shī ma?
你是老师吗?
Are you a teacher?

Answer:
_____
_____
_____

Dialogue 5:
Nǐ shì xué sheng ma?
你是学生吗?
Are you a student?
Answer:

_____
_____
_____
_____

Initials and Finals

Identify the initials and finals in the following words. Practice them by enunciating their tones correctly. You will also see their English translation, as well as their Chinese characters next to the pinyin.

Pinyin	Chinese character(s)	English
Xiū xi	休息	Rest
Xīng qī	星期	Week
Jī jí	积极	Positive
Jī qì	机器	Machine
Xiāng jiāo	香蕉	Banana
Xìng qù	兴趣	Interests
Xiǎo qū	小区	Community
Jì xù	继续	Carry on
Xǐ zǎo	洗澡	To shower/bathe
Dǎ sǎo	打扫	Clean up
Zuó tiān	昨天	Yesterday
Zǎo shang	早上	Morning
Sān cì	三次	Three times

Cāo chǎng	操场	Playground
Zì jǐ	自己	Self
Hán zì	汉字	Chinese characters

Mandarin Teacher

Context Specific Dialogue

Dialogue 1: Asking whether an Individual is your Mandarin teacher.

Person A:	Who is she?
　　　　　　她是谁?
　　Tā shì shéi?

Person B:	She is my Mandarin teacher. Her name is Mei Yong.
　　　　　　她是我的中文老师。她的名字叫美咏。
　　　　　　Tā shì wǒ de zhōng wén lǎo shī. Tā de míng zì jiào Mei Yong.

Non-Context Specific Dialogues

Dialogue 2: Asking about where someone comes from.

Person A: Which country are you from?
你来自哪个国家?
Nǐ lái zì nǎ ge guó jiā?

Person B: The United States of America. What about you?
美国。你呢?
Měi Guó. Nǐ ne?

Person A: I am from China.
我来自中国。
Wǒ lái zì Zhōng Guó.

Dialogue 3: Asking the relationship of one person to another.

Person A: Who is he?
他是谁?
Tā shì shéi?

Person B: He is my classmate.
他是我同学。
Tā shì wǒ tóng xué.

Person A: What about her? Is she your classmate?
那她呢? 她是你同学吗?
Nà tā ne? Tā shì nǐ tóng xué ma?

Person B: No, she is not. She is my friend.
不, 她不是。 她是我朋友。
Bù, tā bù shì. Tā shì wǒ péng yǒu.

Practice Dialogues

Complete and answer the following questions which are in pinyin. If you get stuck, refer back to the notes and previous chapters in order to solidify your knowledge.

Dialogue 1:

Nǐ shì nǎ guó rén?

你是哪国人?

Which country are you from?

Answer:

Dialogue 2:

Nǐ jiào shén me míng zi?

你叫什么名字?

What is your name?

Answer:

Dialogue 3:

Nǐ de Hàn yǔ lǎo shī shì nǎ guó rén?

你的汉语老师是哪国人?

Which country is your Mandarin teacher from?

Answer:

Dialogue 4.

Nǐ de Hàn yǔ lǎo shī jiào shén me míng zi?

你的汉语老师叫什么名字?

What is the name of your Mandarin teacher?

Answer:

Dialogue 5:

Nǐ de Zhōng Guó péng you shì shéi?

你的中国朋友是谁?

Who is your Chinese friend?

Answer:
_____
_____
_____
_____
___

Initials and Finals

Identify the initials and finals in the following words. Practice them by enunciating their tones correctly. You will also see their English translation as well as their Chinese characters next to the pinyin.

Pinyin	Chinese character(s)	English
Zhī shì	知识	Knowledge
Rèn shì	认识	Recognize
Rán shāo	燃烧	Burn
Shǒu shù	手术	Surgery
Chú shī	厨师	Chef
Cháng shì	常识	General knowledge
Rè nào	热闹	Lively
Shāng chǎng	商场	Mall
Shēng rì	生日	Birthday
Shì shí	事实	Truth
Chū chāi	出差	Business trip
Chāo shì	超市	Supermarket
Shàng Chē	上车	Enter the car
Chāo rén	超人	Superman
Cháng chéng	长城	The Great Wall of China

| Chōng zhí | 充值 | Recharge |

Family, Age and Complex Numbers

Context Specific Dialogues

Dialogue 1: Asking the amount of people in another's family.

Person A: How many people are there in your family?
   你家有几口人?
   Nǐ jiā yǒu jǐ kǒu rén?
Person B: There are four.
   我有四个。
   Wǒ yǒu sì gè.

Dialogue 2: Asking how old one's daughter is.

Person A: How old is your daughter?
   你女儿多大了?
   Nǐ nǚ ér duō dà le?
Person B: She is four years old.
   她四岁了。
   Tā sì suì le.

Non-Context Specific Dialogue

Dialogue 3: Asking about the relatives of another person.

Person A: How old is Professor Li?
   李教授几岁了?
   Lǐ jiào shòu jǐ suì le?
Person B: She is 50 years old.
   她五十岁了。
   Tā wǔ shí suì le.
Person A: What about her daughter?
   那她女儿呢?
   Nà tā nǚ ér ne?

Person B: Her daughter is 20.

她二十岁了。

Tā èr shí suì le.

Practice Dialogues

These practice dialogues will test your ability to have solidified your current knowledge. If you get stuck, feel free to revisit the previous chapters. Make sure that all the information and knowledge in these first two chapters are fully understood, as they will be teased out in more detail as the book progresses.

Dialogue 1:

Nǐ jiā yǒu jǐ kǒu rén?

你家有几口人?

How many people are there in your family?

Answer:

_____
_____
_____
_____

___

Dialogue 2:

Nǐ jīn nián duō dà le?

你今年多大了?

How old are you this year?

Answer:

_____
_____
_____
_____

___

Dialogue 3:

Nǐ de Hàn yǔ lǎo shī jīn nián duō dà le?

你的汉语老师今年几岁了?

How old is your Mandarin teacher this year?

Answer:

_____
_____

Dialogue 4:

Nǐ de Zhōng Guó péng you jiā yǒu jǐ kǒu rén?

你的中国朋友家有几口人?

How many people are there in your Chinese friend's family?

Answer:

Dialogue 5:

Nǐ de Zhōng Guó péng you jīn nián duō dà le?

你的中国朋友今年多大了?

How old is your Chinese friend this year?

Answer:

Age and Numbers

Learning how to count from one to ten creates a very good foundation when learning the intricacies of numbers in Mandarin. However, when asking and receiving questions regarding age, it is important to understand how the numbers that express an age are derived in Mandarin.

The table below will give you a very simple approach to constructing the different numbers in pinyin. It uses two main axes with one through ten being on the horizontal axis and factors of ten on the vertical axis. Following these axes to a specific number in the table will allow you to visually see how a specific number is pronounced, as well as how the pinyin was constructed. Take a look below:

	1 yī	2 èr	3 sān	4 sì	5 wǔ	6 liù	7 qī	8 bā	9 jiǔ
10 shí	11 shí yī	12 shí èr	13 shí sān	14 shí sì	15 shí wǔ	16 shí liù	17 shí qī	18 shí bā	19 shí jiǔ
20 èr shí	21 èr shí yī	22 èr shí èr	23 èr shí sān	24 èr shí sì	25 èr shí wǔ	26 èr shí liù	27 èr shí qī	28 èr shí bā	29 èr shí jiǔ
30 sān shí	31 sān shí yī	32 sān shí èr	33 sān shí sān	34 sān shí sì	35 sān shí wǔ	36 sān shí liù	37 sān shí qī	38 sān shí bā	39 sān shí jiǔ
40 sì shí	41 sì shí yī	42 sì shí èr	43 sì shí sān	44 sì shí sì	45 sì shí wǔ	46 sì shí liù	47 sì shí qī	48 sì shí bā	49 sì shí jiǔ
50 wǔ shí	51 wǔ shí yī	52 wǔ shí èr	53 wǔ shí sān	54 wǔ shí sì	55 wǔ shí wǔ	56 wǔ shí liù	57 wǔ shí qī	58 wǔ shí bā	59 wǔ shí jiǔ
60	61	62	63	64	65	66	67	68	69

liù shí	liù shí yī	liù shí èr	liù shí sān	liù shí sì	liù shí wǔ	liù shí liù	liù shí qī	liù shí bā	liù shí jiǔ
70 qī shí	71 qī shí yī	72 qī shí èr	73 qī shí sān	74 qī shí sì	75 qī shí wǔ	76 qī shí liù	77 qī shí qī	78 qī shí bā	79 qī shí jiǔ
80 bā shí	81 bā shí yī	82 bā shí èr	83 bā shí sān	84 bā shí sì	85 bā shí wǔ	86 bā shí liù	87 bā shí qī	88 bā shí bā	89 bā shí jiǔ
90 jiǔ shí	91 jiǔ shí yī	92 jiǔ shí èr	93 jiǔ shí sān	94 jiǔ shí sì	95 jiǔ shí wǔ	96 jiǔ shí liù	97 jiǔ shí qī	98 jiǔ shí bā	99 jiǔ shí jiǔ

Now that you have the different pinyin translations for the English numbers, it is time to correlate them to translated Chinese characters. Using the amount of Chinese characters associated with each number below, try to divide the above pinyin into segments that represent the number in question. This will allow you to train your eye in being able to recognize and read syllables. The Chinese character translations for the above pinyin are as follows:

	1 一	**2** 二	**3** 三	**4** 四	**5** 五	**6** 六	**7** 七	**8** 八	**9** 九
10 十	11 十一	12 十二	13 十三	14 十四	15 十五	16 十六	17 十七	18 十八	19 十九
20 二十	21 二十一	22 二十二	23 二十三	24 二十四	25 二十五	26 二十六	27 二十七	28 二十八	29 二十九
30 三十	31 三十一	32 三十二	33 三十三	34 三十四	35 三十五	36 三十六	37 三十七	38 三十八	39 三十九
40 四十	41 四十一	42 四十二	43 四十三	44 四十四	45 四十五	46 四十六	47 四十七	48 四十八	49 四十九
50 五十	51 五十一	52 五十二	53 五十三	54 五十四	55 五十五	56 五十六	57 五十七	58 五十八	59 五十九
60 六十	61 六十一	62 六十二	63 六十三	64 六十四	65 六十五	66 六十六	67 六十七	68 六十八	69 六十九
70 七十	71 七十一	72 七十二	73 七十三	74 七十四	75 七十五	76 七十六	77 七十七	78 七十八	79 七十九
80 八十	81 八十一	82 八十二	83 八十三	84 八十四	85 八十五	86 八十六	87 八十七	88 八十八	89 八十九
90 九十	91 九十一	92 九十二	93 九十三	94 九十四	95 九十五	96 九十六	97 九十七	98 九十八	99 九十九

Now that you have all the necessary translations of the different numbers, try creating your own dialogues. These dialogues can include asking others which number comes after another or enquiring as to the age of another person. The more creative you become, the more fun you will have, and the more fun you have, the better your memory will be of specific information, knowledge, and concepts. With that being said, we have reached the part in the chapter where we give you some new and fun words to learn.

New Words and Phrases

- One hundred
    一百
    Yī bǎi
- Zero
    零
    Líng
- Sing
    唱
    Chàng
- Remember
    记得
    Jì dé
- Introduce
    介绍
    Jiè shào
- Explain
    说明
    Shuō míng
- Climb
    爬
    Pá
- Believe
    相信
    Xiāng xìn
- Child
    孩子
    Há izi
- Older brother

哥哥
Gē gē

- Younger brother

弟弟
Dì dì

- Older sister

姊姊
Jiě jie

- Younger sister

妹妹
Mèi mei

- Son

儿子
Ér zi

- Daughter

女儿
Nǚ ér

- Accept

接受
Jiē shòu

- Borrow

借
Jiè

- Change

更改
Gēng gǎi

- Complete

完成
Wán chéng

- Hide

躲
Duǒ

- Give
  给
  Gěi _____
- Meet
  遇到
  Yù dào _____
- Need
  需要
  Xū yào _____
- Open
  打开
  Dǎ kāi _____
- Look
  看
  Kàn _____
- Speak
  说话
  Shuō huà _____
- Stand
  站
  Zhàn _____
- Study
  读书
  Dú shū _____
- Butterfly
  蝴蝶
  Hú dié _____
- Eagle
  老鹰
  Lǎo yīng _____
- Roots
  树根 _____

Shù gēn　_____

- Lavender

  薰衣草　_____

  Xūn yī cǎo　_____

- Ocean

  海洋

  Hǎi yáng　_____

- Waves

  波浪　_____

  Bō làng　_____

- Beach

  海滩　_____

  Hǎi tān　_____

- Beetroot

  红菜头　_____

  Hóng cài tóu　_____

- Bell pepper

  灯笼椒　_____

  Dēng lóng jiāo　_____

- Pasta

  意大利面条　_____

  Yì dà lì miàn tiáo　_____

- Doughnuts

  甜甜圈　_____

  Tián tián quān　_____

- How have you been?

  你最近好吗?　_____

  Nǐ zuì jìn hǎo ma?　_____

- Good morning

  早安　_____

  Zǎo ān　_____

- Good afternoon

午安 _____
Wǔ ān _____

- Good evening/good night

    晚安 _____

    Wǎ nān _____

- Pleased to meet you

    高兴认识你 _____

    Gāo xìng rèn shí nǐ _____

- Let us meet soon

    我们再约 _____

    Wǒ men zài yuē _____

Chapter 3: Daily Living

The foundation that you have now built contains information and knowledge that will allow you to survive in a Mandarin-speaking country. However, you do not want to just survive, but thrive. Thus, we will now add some meat to the bones, ensuring that your conversations have substance and that interactions with those who are fluent in Mandarin do not become awkward. The topics may seem rather random in terms of content; however, these are the most common categories of information that should be obtained.

Dates

You want to make sure that you know the months and days of the week. You may find yourself in a situation where someone asks you what day it is, and because you are kind and courteous, you will most likely want to help. That is also a value ingrained within Chinese culture — assisting where you can. With that said, let's dive right in!

Context Specific Dialogues

Dialogue 1: Asking someone what the date and day of the week is.

Person A: Excuse me, what is the date today?

对不起, 请问今天几号?

Duì bùqǐ, qǐngwèn jīn tiān jǐ hào?

Person B: It is December 12th.

十二月十二日。

Shí èr yuè shí èr rì.

Person A: What day is it today?

今天星期几?

Jīn tiān xīng qí jǐ?

Person B: It is Friday.

星期五。

Xīng qí wǔ.

Dialogue 2: Asking the date and day of the week using past and future tenses.

Person A: What was the date yesterday?

昨天是几号?

Zuó tiān shì jǐ hào?

Person B: It was Monday, July 17th.

星期一，七月十七日。

Xīng qí yī, qī yuè shí qī rì.

Person A: What about tomorrow?

那明天呢?

Nà míng tiān ne?

Person B: It is Wednesday, July 19th.

星期三，七月十九日。

Xīng qí sān, qī yuè shí jiǔ rì.

Non-Context Specific Dialogue

Dialogue 3: Asking whether someone will be going to school.

Person A: Tomorrow is Saturday. Will you go to school?

明天是星期六。 你会去学校吗?

Míng tiān shì xīng qí liù. Nǐ huì qù xué xiào ma?

Person B: Yes, I will.

是，我会去。

Shì, wǒ huì qù.

Person A: What are you going to do there?

你会在那里做什么?

Nǐ huì zài nà lǐ zuò shén me?

Person B: I am going there to do some reading.

我要去看书。

Wǒ yào qù kàn shū.

Practice Dialogues

Months and days of the week are easy to understand, but they just need to have their components well understood. Before we jump into the practice dialogues, let's go through what the months and days of the week are when translated into pinyin and their Chinese characters. The months of the year are as follows:

English	Pinyin	Chinese characters
January	yī yuè	一月
February	èr yuè	二月
March	sān yuè	三月
April	sì yuè	四月
May	wǔ yuè	五月
June	liù yuè	六月
July	qī yuè	七月
August	bā yuè	八月
September	jiǔ yuè	九月
October	shí yuè	十月
November	shí yī yuè	十一月
December	shí èr yuè	十二月

As you can see above, there is a very distinct pattern that can be used in order to correctly identify and record the months of the year. The numbers from one to ten have their pinyin included in the respective month from one to ten. As soon as the tenth month is reached (October), the names of 11 and 12 are used. At the end, the word 'yuè' is added to show reference to the name of a month.

We will now delve into the different days of the week. These are as follows:

English	Pinyin	Chinese characters
Monday	xīng qī yī	星期一
Tuesday	xīng qī èr	星期二
Wednesday	xīng qī sān	星期三
Thursday	xīng qī sì	星期四
Friday	xīng qī wǔ	星期五

| Saturday | xīng qī liù | 星期六 |
| Sunday | xīng qī tiān / xīng qī rì | 星期天 / 星期日 |

The naming of the days of the week follow a similar pattern to that of the months of the year. However, the exception is with Sunday. The words 'xīng qī' are used to refer to a day of the week. However, the number seven is also 'qī'. Thus, to avoid confusion, the seventh day of the week (Sunday) has slightly different pinyin and Chinese characters. Now that we have established a good base in terms of dates, months, and days of the week, we can now move on to the practice dialogues.

Dialogue 1:

Jīn tiān jǐ yuè jǐ hào xīng qī jǐ?

今天几月几号星期几?

What is today's month, date, and day?

Answer:

_____
_____
_____
_____

_____

Dialogue 2:

Míng tiān jǐ yuè jǐ hào xīng qī jǐ?

明天几月几号星期几?

What is tomorrow's month, date, and day?

Answer:

_____
_____
_____
_____

_____

Dialogue 3:

Zuó tiān jǐ yuè jǐ hào xīng qī jǐ?

昨天几月几号星期几?

What is yesterday's month, date, and day?

Answer:
_____
_____
_____
_____

Dialogue 4:

Míng tiān nǐ qù nǎr zuò shén me?

明天你去哪做什么?

Where are you going tomorrow, and what will you be doing?

Answer:
_____
_____
_____
_____

Dialogue 5:

Xīng qīrì nǐ qù nǎr zuò shén me ?

星期日你去哪做什么?

Where are you going, and what will you be doing on Sunday?

Answer:
_____
_____
_____
_____

Initials and Finals

Identify the initials and finals in the following words. Practice them by enunciating their tones correctly. You will also see their English translation and Chinese characters next to the pinyin.

Pinyin	Chinese character(s)	English
Guó jiā	国家	Country

Zuó tiān	昨天	Yesterday
Míng tiān	明天	Tomorrow
Nián qīng	年轻	Young
Lóu fáng	楼房	Building
Lán qiú	篮球	Basketball
Míng nián	明年	Next year
Píng guǒ	苹果	Apple
Pí jiǔ	啤酒	Beer
Niú nǎi	牛奶	Milk
Yóu yǒng	游泳	Swim
Huán jìng	环境	Environment
Hán jià	寒假	Winter holiday
Niú ròu	牛肉	Steak
Yóu xì	游戏	Game

Ordering Food and Drink

You will find yourself more times than you might think ordering food and drink from either a restaurant or a night market. The latter is extremely common in native Mandarin-speaking countries. So, to be able to communicate effectively, we thought it would be apt to focus on learning some new terms, whilst revising what was learned in the previous book.

Context Specific Dialogues

Dialogue 1: Ordering something to drink and eat at a restaurant.

Person A: What would you like to drink?

你要喝什么?

Nǐ yào hē shén me?

Person B: I'd like some tea.

我想喝茶。

Wǒ xiǎng hē chá.

Person A: What would you like to eat?

你要吃什么?

Nǐ yào chī shén me?

Person B: I would like some rice please.

我想吃饭。

Wǒ xiǎng chī fàn.

Non-Context Specific Dialogue

Dialogue 2: Answering a question about what you want to buy at a store.

Person A: What would you like to do this afternoon?

你今天下午想做什么?

Nǐ jīn tiān xià wǔ xiǎng zuò shén me?

Person B: I would like to go shopping.

我想去逛街。

Wǒ xiǎng qù guàng jiē.

Person A: What do you want to buy?

你想买什么?

Nǐ xiǎng mǎi shén me?

Person B: I want to buy a cup.

我想买杯子。

Wǒ xiǎng mǎi bēi zi.

Dialogue 3: Asking about the price of items.

Person A: Hello! How much is this cup?

你好! 这杯子多少钱?

Nǐ hǎo, zhè bēi zi duō shǎo qián?

Person B: 28 yuan.

二十八元。

Èr shí bā yuán.

Person A: What about that one?

那这个呢?

Nà zhè ge ne?

Person B: That one is 18 yuan.

那个十八元。

Nà gè shí bā yuán.

Amounts of Money

As with all other countries, Mandarin-speaking countries will use a specific currency. However, it may happen that a specific country may not use the 'yuan' (元) as their currency. It is therefore recommended to do some research regarding the most common currencies that are used in the country that you are planning to visit/emigrate to.

The reason that it is important to learn both the pinyin and Chinese characters for specific values is that a price will not necessarily always have numerical values for you to identify. You may find that the price will be written purely in Chinese characters. To curb any undue anxiety and confusion, here are a few values to note:

English	Pinyin	Chinese characters
One yuan	yī yuan	一元
Five yuan	wǔ yuan	五元
Ten yuan	shí yuan	十元
50 yuan	wǔshí	五十元
100 yuan	yī bǎi yuan	一百元

Practice Dialogues

You are getting closer and closer to being able to operate effectively on your own in any native Mandarin-speaking country. So, to make sure you are up to scratch, why don't you answer the following dialogues based on the questions written in pinyin? We challenge you to write your answer in English, pinyin, and Chinese characters. The practice dialogues that have been prepared for you are as follows:

Dialogue 1:

Nǐ xiǎng chī shén me?

你想吃什么?

What would you like to eat?

Answer:

_____
_____
_____
_____

_____

Dialogue 2:

Nǐ xiǎng hē shén me?

你想喝什么?

What would you like to drink?

Answer:

_____
_____
_____
_____

Dialogue 3:

Míng tiān xià wǔ nǐ xiǎng zuò shén me?

明天下午你想做什么?

What would you like to do tomorrow afternoon?

Answer:

_____
_____
_____
_____

Dialogue 4:

Nǐ qù nǎge shāng diàn mǎi bēi zi?

你去哪个商店买杯子?

You went to that shop to buy a cup?

Answer:

_____
_____
_____
_____

Dialogue 5:

Yí ge bēi zi duō shao qián?

一个杯子多少钱?

How much is a cup?

Answer:
_____
_____
_____
_____
_____

Initials and Finals

Pinyin	Chinese character(s)	English
Lǎo shī	老师	Teacher
Měi tiān	每天	Every day
Hǎ ibiān	海边	Beach
Yǐ jīng	已经	Already
Lǎo rén	老人	Old person
Měi nián	每年	Every year
Hǎi mián	海绵	Sponge
Yǐ qián	以前	Before
Yǔ sǎn	雨伞	Umbrella
Měi hǎo	美好	Beautiful
Xǐ zǎo	洗澡	Shower/bath
Biǎo yǎn	表演	Perform/performance
Yǒu yòng	有用	Useful
Měi lì	美丽	Beautiful
Gǎn xiè	感谢	Gratitude
Biǎo xiàn	表现	Performance

Occupations

One of the typical points of conversation is to ask someone what their occupation is. Not only does this open up the conversation into an array of different avenues in terms of follow-up questions, but it also acts as a filler question when you feel that there is an awkward silence ensuing. Asking about another's occupation can be seen as quite a personal question, so it is important to start off with the appropriate greetings before jumping into more person-specific questions. For now, focus on obtaining the correct pinyin and Chinese character translations.

Context Specific Dialogues

Dialogue 1: Asking where someone works.

Person A: Where do you work?

你在哪里工作?

Nǐ zài nǎlǐ gōng zuò?

Person B: I work in a school.

我在学校工作。

Wǒ zài xué xiào gōng zuò.

Person A: Where does your son work?

你儿子在哪工作?
Nǐ ér zi zài nǎ gōng zuò.

Person B: My son works in a hospital. He is a doctor.
他在医院工作。他是医生。
Tā zài yī yuàn gōng zuò. Tā shì yī shēng.

Non-Context Specific Dialogue

Dialogue 2: Asking where somebody's family member is.

Person A: Is your father at home?
你父亲在家吗?
Nǐ fù qīn zài jiā ma?

Person B: No, he is not.
不, 他不在。
Bù, tā bù zài.

Person A: Where is he?
他在哪?
Tā zài nǎ?

Person B: He is in the hospital.
他在医院。
Tā zài yī yuàn.

Dialogue 3: Asking the whereabouts of one's animals.

Person A: Where is the kitty?
猫咪在哪?
Māo mī zài nǎ?

Person B: The kitty is over there.
猫咪在那。
Māo mī zài nà.

Person A: Where is the puppy?
小狗在哪?
Xiǎo gǒu zài nǎ?

Person B: The puppy is under the chair.

小狗在椅子底下。

Xiǎo gǒu zài yǐ zi dǐ xia.

Based on the non-context specific dialogues, one is able to see how there is a common manner in which we refer to people and animals. The questions remain specific and build on the information and knowledge that you have already obtained in previous chapters. If you find yourself struggling, we encourage you to revisit and revise the previously learned content. Remember that it is okay to forget; re-learning concepts makes you a better student!

Focusing on the context specific dialogue, it is important that we delve a bit deeper into the various types of occupations that exist. Below, you will find a few examples of different occupations, their pinyin, and their corresponding Chinese characters:

English	Pinyin	Chinese characters
Engineer	Gōng chéng shī	工程师
Shopkeeper	Diàn zhǔ	店主
Banker	Yín háng jiā	银行家
Policeman	Jǐng chá	警察
Pilot	Fēi xíng yuán	飞行员
Lawyer	Lǜ shī	律师
Teacher	Lǎo shī	老师
Professor	Jiào shòu	教授
Scientist	Kē xué jiā	科学家
Pharmacist	Yào jì shī	药剂师
Athlete	Yùn dòng yuán	运动员
Dentist	Yá yī	牙医
Accountant	Kuài jì	会计
Driver	Sī jī	司机

Practice Dialogues

These dialogues combine all the context specific and non-context specific dialogues that have been learned thus far. It is a fantastic way to gauge the progress that you have made. At this point in the workbook, it is highly advised that you implement "revision days" into your study timetable. Depending on the pace at which you are studying, more than one revision day may be necessary in order to concretize the information. Examples of dialogues that are related to the 'Occupation' subheading, are as follows:

Dialogue 1:

Xiǎo gǒu zài nǎr?

小狗在哪?

Where is the puppy?

Answer:

_____
_____
_____
_____

_____

Dialogue 2:

Tā zài nǎr gōng zuò?

他在哪工作?

Where is he working?

Answer:

_____
_____
_____
_____

_____

Dialogue 3:

Tā ér zi zài nǎr gōng zuò?

他儿子在哪工作?

Where is his son working?

Answer:
_____
_____
_____
_____
_____

Dialogue 4:
Tā bà ba zài jiā ma?
她爸爸在家吗?
Is her dad at home?
Answer:
_____
_____
_____
_____
_____

Dialogue 5:
Tā bà ba zài nǎr ne?
她爸爸在哪呢?
Where is her dad?
Answer:
_____
_____
_____
_____
_____

Initials and Finals

Pinyin	Chinese character(s)	English
Xià tiān	夏天	Summer
Diàn dēng	电灯	Electric light
Chàng gē	唱歌	Sing

Jiàn kāng	健康	Healthy
Qù nián	去年	Last year
Diàn chí	电池	Battery
Fù xí	复习	Revise
Dì tú	地图	Map
Tiào wǔ	跳舞	Dance
Diàn yǐng	电影	Movie
Hàn yǔ	汉语	Mandarin Chinese
Dì tiě	地铁	Subway
Shuì jiào	睡觉	Sleep
Diàn shì	电视	Television
Hàn zì	汉字	Chinese characters
Jiàn miàn	见面	Meet

Actions and Questions

When wanting to ask for assistance, or to use a chair that is at someone's table, it is important that the correct vocabulary is used. Not only should the request resemble a question to prompt an answer, but the question needs to be well understood so that the other person can give an accurate answer. It is human nature to be inquisitive, which means that you may find yourself asking questions to someone about someone else. This can be a fantastic way to strategize for a conversation that you may want to have with that person.

Whether it be asking to sit in a communal area or inquiring as to what objects are present on different surfaces, we will be covering many different actions and questions that are commonly utilized during one's daily life.

Context Specific Dialogues

Dialogue 1: Asking whether a seat is taken.

Person A: Is this seat taken?

                  这座位有人坐了吗?
                  Zhè zuò wèi yǒu rén zuò le ma?

Person B: No it is not.
不, 没有。
Bù, méi yǒu.

Person A: Can I sit here?
我可以坐着吗?
Wǒ kě yǐ zuò zhe ma?

Person B: Yes, please.
可以, 请。
Kě yǐ, qǐng.

Dialogue 2: Asking information about others.

Person A: Who is the person in the front?
前头那个人是谁?
Qián tou nà gè rén shì shéi?

Person B: She is Wang Yang. She works in a hospital.
她是王梅。她在医院工作。
Tā shì wáng méi. Tā zài yī yuàn gōng zuò.

Person A: What about the person at the back? What is his name?
那后头那个人呢? 他叫什么名字?
Nà hòu tou nà gè rén ne? Tā jiào shén me míng zì?

Person B: He is Xie Zhang. He works in a store.
他叫谢长。他在店里工作。
Tā jiào xiè zhǎng. Tā zài diàn lǐ gōng zuò.

Dialogue 3: Asking about where an object is.

Person A: What is there on that desk?
桌上有什么?
Zhuō shàng yǒu shén me?

Person B: There is a computer and a book.
有一台电脑和一本书。

Yǒu yī tái diàn nǎo hé yī běn shū.

Person A: Where is the cup?

杯子在哪?

Bēi zi zài nǎ?

Person B: It is in the drawer of the desk.

在桌子的抽屉里。

Zài zhuō zi de chōu tì lǐ.

Practice Dialogues

The objects that are present in these dialogues can be substituted with other everyday objects. The sentence will still make sense after the object swap has occurred. For example, if one were to say, "Where is the cup?" and were to substitute "cup" with "knife" by simply using the Chinese character for "knife" with that of the one for "cup", the sentence would be complete and perfectly understood by anyone who has studied Mandarin.

Let's try some practice dialogues to delve deeper into possible sentence structures. The examples are as follows:

Dialogue 1:

Diàn nǎo zài nǎr?

电脑在哪?

Where is the computer?

Answer:

_____

_____

_____

_____

_____

Dialogue 2:

Shū zài nǎr?

书在哪?

Where is the book?

Answer:

_____

Dialogue 3:

Zhuō zi lǐmiàn yǒu shén me?

桌子里面有什么?

What is inside the table?

Answer:

Dialogue 4:

Nǎ ge rén shì Wáng Fāng?

那个人是王芳吗?

Is that person Wang Fang?

Answer:

Dialogue 5:

Nǎ ge rén shì Xiè Péng?

那个人是谢鹏?

Is that person Xie Peng?

Answer:

Initials and Finals

The initials and finals, which you should be able to identify below, act as an extensive list of common terms of reference to other people and objects. Thus, it is important for you to spend sufficient time learning these pinyin, as well as the very subtle differences with their correlated Chinese characters.

Pinyin	Chinese character(s)	English
Bà ba	爸爸	Dad
Gē ge	哥哥	Older brother
Gū gu	姑姑	Aunt (father's side)
Xiè xie	谢谢	Thank you
Mā ma	妈妈	Mom
Jiě jie	姐姐	Older sister
Shū shu	叔叔	Uncle (father's younger brother)
Kàn kan	看看	Look
Yé ye	爷爷	Grandfather (paternal)
Dì di	弟弟	Younger brother
Tài tai	太太	Wife
Shuō shuo	说说	Say
Nǎi nai	奶奶	Grandmother (paternal)
Mèi mei	妹妹	Younger sister
Xīng xing	星星	Stars
Cháng chang	常常	Often
Nǐ men	你们	You guys
Zhuō zi	桌子	Table
Shé tou	舌头	Tongue

Qián tou	前头	In front
Wǒ men	我们	Us
Yǐ zi	椅子	Chair
Zhěn tou	枕头	Pillow
Hòu tou	后头	Behind
Tā men	他们	Them
Bēi zi	杯子	Cup
Shí tou	石头	Stone
Lǐ tou	里头	Inside
Rén men	人们	People
Bèi zi	被子	Blanket
Mù tou	木头	Wood log
Wài tou	外头	Outside

Time

Being able to tell the time in Mandarin is vital. Not only might there be instances when clock faces show only the Chinese characters when telling time, but in terms of conversation, it is one of the most commonly asked questions to date. Whether you plan on reading time numerically or switching over to Chinese characters, it is important to spend some time on this section. Let's start with some context specific dialogues.

Context Specific Dialogues

Dialogue 1: Asking what the time is.

Person A: What is the time now?

现在几点?

Xiàn zài jǐ diǎn?

Person B: It is ten past ten.

现在十点十分。

Xiàn zài shí diǎn shí fēn.

Person A: When shall we have our lunch?

我们几点吃午餐?

Wǒ men jǐ diǎn chī wǔ cān?

Person B:		At 12 o'clock.

十二点。

Shí èr diǎn.

Dialogue 2: Asking when someone will be returning.

Person A:		When is father coming home?

父亲什么时候回家?

Fù qīn shén me shí hòu huí jiā?

Person B:		At five o'clock this afternoon.

下午五点。

Xià wǔ wǔ diǎn.

Person A:		When are we going to see the movie?

我们什么时候去看点电影?

Wǒ men shén me shí hòu qù kàn diǎn diàn yǐng?

Person B:		At half past six.

六点半。

Liù diǎn bàn.

Dialogue 3: Asking when someone will be departing and returning to an area.

Person A:		I'll go to Beijing next Tuesday.

我下星期二要去北京。

Wǒ xià xīng qí èr yào qù Běijīng.

Person B:		How long will you stay in Beijing?

你要在北京待多久?

Nǐ yào zài běi jīng dài duō jiǔ?

Person A:		For four days.

四天。

Sì tiān.

Person B:		Can you come back before Friday?

你能星期五前回来吗?

Nǐ néng xīng qí wǔ qián huí lái ma?

Person A:		Yes, I can.

我可以。

Wǒ kě yǐ.

Telling the Time

Many will look at their watches or living room clocks and successfully be able to tell the time in English. However, what if someone is visiting and they ask you what the time is? Do you shy back into your comfort zone and answer in English? No, you remain confident in your abilities because you've studied Mandarin to this point, and you try to say it in Mandarin, even if you end up making mistakes.

To help you on your journey in becoming confident in telling the time in Madarin, here is a breakdown of different times and how they are translated into pinyin and Chinese characters.

English	Pinyin	Chinese characters
One o'clock	Yī diǎn	一点
Two o'clock	Liǎng diǎn	两点
Three o'clock	Sān diǎn	三点
Four o'clock	Sì diǎn	四点
Five o'clock	Wǔ diǎn	五点
Six o'clock	Liù Diǎn	六点
Seven o'clock	Qī Diǎn	七点
Eight o'clock	Bā Diǎn	八点
Nine o'clock	Jiǔ Diǎn	九点
Ten o'clock	Shí Diǎn	十点
11 o'clock	Shí yī Diǎn	十一点
12 o'clock	Shí èr Diǎn	十二点
Quarter past	...Shí wǔ Fēn	...十五分
Half past	...Bàn/Sān shí Fēn	...半/三十分
Quarter to	...Sì shí wǔ Fēn	...四十五分

Morning	Zăo shang	早上
Afternoon	Zhōng wǔ	中午
Evening	Wăn shàng	晚上
Midnight	Bàn yè	半夜

Let's really absorb the above information by tackling a few examples. Write the English times below in both pinyin and its respective Chinese characters. Take some time to rewrite the pinyin and Chinese characters in the spaces provided.

- Quarter past ten
    十点十五分   _____
    Shí diăn shí wǔ fēn   _____

- Quarter to two
    一点四十五分   _____
    Yī diăn sì shí wǔ fēn   _____

- Five o'clock in the afternoon
    下午五点   _____
    Xià wǔ wǔ diăn   _____

- 2:45 AM
    凌晨两点四十五分   _____
    Líng chén liăng diăn sì shí wǔ fēn _____

- Quarter to midnight
    晚上十一点四十五分   _____
    Wăn shàng shí yī diăn sì shí wǔ fēn _____

- Half past four in the afternoon
    下午四点半   _____
    Xià wǔ sì diăn bàn   _____

- Quarter past seven
    七点十五分   _____
    Qī diăn shí wǔ fēn   _____

- 5:00 AM

- 早上五点
  Zǎo shang wǔ diǎn
- 11:30 AM
  早上十一点半
  Zǎo shang shí yī diǎn bàn
- Nine o'clock in the evening
  晚上九点
  Wǎn shàng jiǔ diǎn

Practice Dialogues

Focusing on the information that was just learned and combining it with the context specific dialogues, try your hand at the following practice dialogues. This specific set focuses on applying what you have learned and integrating it with common sentence structure, which you should have absorbed by this point. The practice examples that we would like you to complete are as follows:

Dialogue 1:

Xiàn zài jǐdiǎn?

现在几点?

What is the time?

Answer:

_____
_____
_____
_____

_____

Dialogue 2:

Tā men jǐdiǎn chī fàn?

他们几点吃饭?

What time do they eat?

Answer:

_____
_____
_____

Dialogue 3:

Bà ba shén me shí hou huí jiā?

爸爸什么时候回家?

What time does dad get home?

Answer:

_____
_____
_____
_____

Dialogue 4:

Tā men shén me shí hou qù kàn diàn yǐng?

他们什么时候去看电影?

What time will they go watch a movie?

Answer:

_____
_____
_____
_____

Dialogue 5:

Tā qù nǎr? Shén me shí hou néng huí jiā?

他去哪? 什么时候能回家?

Where did he go? What time will he be able to go home?

Answer:

_____
_____
_____
_____

Weather

At some point, you may have started to completely immerse yourself in your journey to learn Mandarin. This may even include watching Chinese news. This is a fantastic method for testing your level of conversational Mandarin. Furthermore, you want to ensure that you are able to understand a bit of what is being said. If you plan on visiting or living in a native Mandarin-speaking country, you will need to learn the basics in terms of understanding the weather. Naturally, being able to read weather forecasts will enable you to plan your days ahead, especially if you commute to in-person Mandarin classes. Let's start off with a few dialogues to get the ball rolling.

Context Specific Dialogues

Dialogue 1: Asking how the weather is in Beijing.

Person A: How was the weather in Beijing yesterday?

昨天北京的天气怎么样？

Zuó tiān běi jīng de tiān qì zěn me yàng?

Person B: It was too hot.

太热了。

	Tài rè le.
Person A:	What about tomorrow? What will the weather be like tomorrow?
	那明天呢？明天天气怎么样？
	Nà míng tiān ne? Míng tiān tiān qì zěn me yàng?
Person B:	It will be fine. Neither hot nor cold.
	还好。不热也不冷。
	Hái hǎo. Bù rè yě bù lěng.

Dialogue 2: Asking about the current day's weather.

Person A:	Will it rain today?
	今天会下雨吗？
	Jīn tiān huì xià yǔ ma?
Person B:	No, it will not rain.
	不，不会下雨。
	Bù, bù huì xià yǔ.
Person A:	Will Miss Wang come today?
	王小姐今天回来吗？
	Wáng xiǎo jiě jīn tiān huí lái ma?
Person B:	No, she will not. It is too cold.
	不，她不会。太冷了。
	Bù, tā bù huì. Tài lěng le.

Non-Context Specific Dialogue

Dialogue 3: Relaying to another person how the weather is making you feel.

Person A:	How are you?
	你好吗？
	Nǐ hǎo ma?
Person B:	Not very well. It is too hot, and I have no appetite.
	不太好。太热了而且我也没胃口。
	Bù tài hǎo. Tài rè le ér qiě wǒ yě méi wèi kǒu.
Person A:	You should eat more fruit and drink more water.

你应该要多吃水果多喝水。

Nǐ yīng gāi yào duō chī shuǐguǒ duō hē shuǐ.

Person B: Thank you, Doctor. I will do this.

谢谢医生。我会这么做。

Xiè xiè yī shēng. Wǒ huì zhè me zuò.

The Different Types of Weather

It is important that the different weather conditions are well understood, especially so that you can communicate effectively with other Mandarin-speaking individuals. Due to the very specific climate that Asian countries experience, it is important to familiarize yourself with those conditions that are not common in your country, as that will be what you experience if you plan to visit or emigrate to a native Mandarin-speaking country. A few examples of different weather conditions are as follows:

English	Pinyin	Chinese characters
Sun	Tài yáng	太阳
Rain	Xià Yǔ	下雨
Hail	Xià Bīng báo	下冰雹
Thunder	Dǎ léi	打雷
Lightning	Shǎn diàn	闪电
Cloudy	Yīn chén	阴沉
Haze	Yīn mái	阴霾
Mist	Wù	雾
Windy	Yǒu Fēng	有风

Practice Dialogues

Using the above, answer the following dialogues as you have previously. This is the last chapter that is loaded with information. Therefore, please ensure that you thoroughly revise all of the information up until this point. The reason for this is that the following chapters will include purely reading and writing exercises. With that being said, here are the practice dialogues based on the 'weather' portion of this chapter:

Dialogue 1:

Zuó tiān Běijīng de tiān qì zěn me yàng?

昨天北京的天气怎么样?

How was the weather in Beijing yesterday?

Answer:

_____
_____
_____
_____

_____

Dialogue 2:

Míng tiān tiān qì zěn me yàng?

明天天气怎么样?

How will the weather be tomorrow?

Answer:

_____
_____
_____
_____

_____

Dialogue 3:

Jīn tiān huì xià yǔ ma?

今天会下雨吗?

Will it rain today?

Answer:

_____
_____
_____
_____

_____

Dialogue 4:

Wáng Xiǎo jiě huí lái ma?

王小姐回来吗?

Will Miss Wang come back today?

Answer:
_____
_____
_____
_____

_____

Dialogue 5:

Tā de shē ntǐ zěn me yàng?

她的身体怎么样?

How is her body?

Answer:
_____
_____
_____
_____

_____

Chapter 4: Reading and Writing

Well done! You have made it this far, and we are super proud of you for it. At this point, you should have a solid foundation of knowledge to successfully hold a conversation in Mandarin. It does not matter how basic the conversation is as you are further than where you initially started. However, although speech is important, it is not the sole use of Mandarin. You will be reading books in Mandarin, as well as trying your best to correlate the pinyin to its respective Chinese characters and even to English. This is why we have prepared a few short stories for you to read. These short stories will be supplied in English, pinyin, and Chinese characters. There will even be some fun questions that will help your comprehension skills.

As you read these short stories, identify the different pinyin, listen to your tones as you pronounce them, and circle any characters that you have not yet learned. You can link this character to its pinyin by following the syllables in the sentence, and then research it accordingly. What a way to continually boost your vocabulary, right? Get ready to build on your foundation, because this is where major strides will be made.

Reading Exercises

When we are practicing our reading, it is important that we are able to correlate the English words with their pinyin and corresponding Chinese characters. This is why the short stories that we have devised for you below contain content that has already been covered in either this workbook or in the first book. If you find yourself struggling, try moving a few characters backwards to one that you recognize. Match that character with the pinyin, then with the English translation in order to clarify the meaning of the passage and to add more knowledge to your repertoire. The questions that follow each short story will be based on the story, with answers being clear and to the point.

Short Story 1

Li Yang is a seven-year-old girl who felt very hungry one day. After she went to go and ask her mother what they were having for dinner, she was sent to go buy some bread. Li left the house and saw that the sun was shining even though the weather forecast had said it would rain. Li got to the store, bought some bread from the storekeeper, and on her way home, she saw her brother. Her brother's name is Xiang Yang, and he was also on his way home. They decided to walk together. When Li got home, she gave the bread to her mother, and that evening the family enjoyed sandwiches for dinner.

杨丽是个七岁小女孩，有一天她感觉很饿。她去问她妈妈晚餐吃什么之后被派去买些面包。丽离开家时外头太阳很耀眼，即使气象报告有说会下雨。丽到了商店后，跟店主买了些面包，回家路上碰见了她哥哥。她哥哥叫扬翔，也在回家路上。她们决定一起走回家。丽回家时把面包交给了她妈妈然后当晚晚餐时家人享受了三明治。

Yáng Lì shì gè qī suì xiǎo nǚ hái, yǒu yī tiān tā gǎn jué hěn è. Tā qù wèn tā mā mā wǎn cān chī shén me zhī hòu bèi pài qù mǎi xiē miàn bāo. Lì lí kāi jiā shí wài tou tài yáng hěn yào yǎn, jí shǐ qì xiàng bào gào yǒu shuō huì xià yǔ. Lì dào le shāng diàn hòu, gēn diàn zhǔ mǎi le xiē miàn bāo, huí jiā lù shàng pèng jiàn le tā gē gē. Tā gē gē jiào Yáng Xiáng, yě zài huí jiā lù shàng. Tā men jué dìng yī qǐ zǒu huí jiā. Lì huí jiā shí bǎ miàn bāo jiāo gěi le tā mā mā rán hòu dàng wǎn wǎn cān shí jiā rén xiǎng shòu le sān míng zhì.

Questions:

Who is Li Yang's brother?/ 杨丽的哥哥是谁?/ Yáng Lì dí gē gē shì shéi?

_____
_____
_____
_____

What did Li Yang's family eat for dinner?/ 杨丽的家人晚餐吃什么?/ Yáng Lì de jiā rén wǎn cān chī shén me?

_____
_____
_____
_____

What weather did Li Yang encounter as she went to the shop?/ 杨丽去商店时是什么天气?/ Yáng Lì qù shāng diàn shí shì shén me tiān qì?

_____
_____
_____
_____

Short Story 2

Chenguang Liu is a 14-year-old boy who wanted to become a doctor when he grew up. His mother and father supported his decision and made sure that he was studying hard. He sat at his desk one night looking at the stars and moon in the sky. Although it was raining, he could see the stars all gathered together. At one moment, he saw a shooting star. Chenguang was so happy that he saw it and immediately made a wish. He wished that one day he would fulfill his dream of becoming a doctor. As time went on, Chenguang studied very hard. Four years later, he wrote his college entrance exams and got a seat in a top college in China. He was making his dreams a reality.

刘 晨光是一 个 十四 岁 的男孩, 他 长 大想要成 为 一名 医 生。他爸爸 妈妈 支持他的 决 定 还 确保他用功 读书 。有一天 晚 上他坐在他的书桌时仰望着夜空的星星与月亮。虽然在下雨,他还是看的到星星聚集。突然他看到了一颗流星。晨光看见了很开兴还立刻许愿。他希望有一天能梦想成真成为一名医生。随着时间流动,晨光依然的用功读书。四年后他写了高考还得到中国顶尖大学的一个位子。他正在实现他的梦想。

Liú Chén Guāng shì yī gè shí sì suì de nán hái, tā zhǎng dà xiǎng yào chéng wéi yī míng yī shēng. Tā bà ba mā mā zhī chí tā de jué dìng hái què bǎo tā yòng gōng dús hū. Yǒu yī tiān wǎn shàng tā zuò zài tā de shū zhuō shí yǎng wàng zhe yè kōng de xīng xīng yǔ yuè liàng. Suī rán zài xià yǔ, tā hái shì kàn de dào xīng xīng jù jí. Tú rán tā kàn dào le yī kē liú xīng. Chén Guāng kàn jiàn le hěn kāi xìng hái lì kè xǔyuàn. Tā xī wàng yǒu yī tiān néng mèng xiǎng chéng zhēn chéng wéi yī míng yī shēng. Suí zhe shí jiān liú dòng, Chén Guāng yī rán de yòng gōng dú shū. Sì nián hòu tā xi ěle gāo kǎo hái dé dào Zhōng Guó dǐng jiān dà xué de yī gè wèi zi. Tā zhèng zài shí xiàn tā de mèng xiǎng.

Questions:

How old is Chenguang Liu?/ 刘晨光几岁?/ Liú Chén Guāng jǐ suì?

_____
_____
_____

How many years was it until Chenguang could take the college entrance exams?/ 晨光几年后才能高考?/ Chén Guāng jǐ nián hòu cái néng gāo kǎo?

_____
_____
_____

What did Chenguang dream of becoming?/ 晨光有梦想成真吗?/ Chén Guāng yǒu mèng xiǎng chéng zhēn ma?

Short Story 3

Dong Hai Zhang was told that on Tuesday he needed to bring his parents to school for show-and-tell. His teacher had given each student a chance to bring their parents in and let the class know what their occupation is. Dong Hai's mother is a dentist, and his father is an engineer. His parents had to be at school at two o'clock in the afternoon. Dong Hai felt rather nervous that his parents were coming to meet his classmates and speak about their jobs. As Dong Hai was sitting in class at a quarter to two in the afternoon, he knew that his parents would be there soon. His feeling of nervousness became excitement as his parents had never been to his school before. Once his parents had given their speech, Dong Hai was allowed to go home with them. This was one of the most special days that Dong Hai will remember forever.

张东海被告知说他星期二需要带他的爸爸妈妈到学校来。他老师给每个学生一个把爸爸妈妈带来和全班介绍他们的职业的机会。东海的妈妈是一名牙医，他爸爸是一名工程师。他爸爸妈妈需要下午两点到学校。他爸爸妈妈要在他同学们讲述他们的职业让东海感觉蛮紧张的。下午一点四十五分的时候东海在教室里坐着，他以知他爸爸妈妈已经快到了。他的紧张感变成了激动应为他爸爸妈妈从来没有来过他学校。当他爸爸妈妈演讲完之后，东海被允许跟他们回家。这是一个最特别的日子让东海永生难忘。

Zhāng Dōng Hǎi bèi gào zhī shuō tā xīng qí èr xū yào dài tā de bà ba mā mā dào xué xiào lái. Tā lǎo shī gěi měi gè xué shēng yī gè bǎ bà ba mā mā dài lái hé quán bān jiè shào tā men de zhí yè de jī huì. Dōng Hǎi de mā mā shì yī míng yá yī, tā bà ba shì yī míng gōng chéng shī. Tā bà ba mā mā xū yào xià wǔ liǎng diǎn dào xué xiào. Tā bà ba mā mā yào zài tā tóng xué men jiǎng shù tā men de zhí yè ràng Dōng Hǎi gǎn jué mán jǐn zhāng de. Xià wǔ yī diǎn sì shí wǔ fēn de shí hòu Dōng Hǎi zài jiào shì lǐ zuò zhe, tā yǐ zhī tā bà ba mā mā yǐ jīng kuài dào le. Tā de jǐn zhāng gǎn biàn chéng le jī dòng yīng wèi tā bà ba mā mā cóng lái méi yǒu lái guò tā xué xiào. Dāng tā bà ba mā mā yǎn jiǎng wán zhī hòu, Dōng Hǎi bèi yǔn xǔ gēn tā men huí jiā. Zhè shì yī gè zuì tè bié de rì zi ràng Dōng Hǎi yǒng shēng nán wàng.

Questions:

What occupations does Dong Hai's parents do?/ 东海的爸爸妈妈的职业是什么?/ Dōng Hǎi de bà ba mā mā de zhí yè shì shén me?

_____
_____
_____
_____

What time did Dong Hai's parents have to be at school?/ 东海的爸爸妈妈什么时间要到学校?/ Dōng Hǎi de bà ba mā mā shén me shí jiān yào dào xué xiào?

_____
_____
_____
_____

What day did Dong Hai's parents come to his school?/东海的爸爸妈妈星期几要到他的学校?/Dōng Hǎi de bà ba mā mā xīng qí jǐ yào dào tā de xué xiào?

_____
_____
_____

Writing Exercises

By this point, you should feel rather comfortable with reading segments of pinyin and Chinese characters and being able to relate them to their English counterparts. This skill will not be perfected overnight and will require a large amount of time and effort. However, in this subsection, we are going to focus on writing. In this section, sentences in both English and Chinese characters will be provided. Your job is to write the pinyin in the space below each sentence. If you see a Chinese character that you do not know in pinyin, do a quick online search in order to add this extra knowledge to your repertoire.

1. When I visited Australia, I was shocked to see kangaroos roaming freely in the wild.

当我去澳大利亚时，看到袋鼠自由漫游时然我感到惊讶。

_____
_____
_____
_____

2. I struggle to fall asleep at night. The main reason for this is that I am always hearing mosquitos.

我很难在晚上入眠。最大的理由是应为我都一直听到蚊子的声音。

_____
_____
_____
_____

3. When I grow up, I want to be a singer. However, my parents think that being a lawyer is a better job for me.

我长大时相当一个歌手。可是我父母觉得当律师是一个对我比较好的职业。

_____

4. I really cannot concentrate when people speak to me when I have to study.
当我需要看书时当其他人跟我讲话时我无法专注。

_____

5. Sometimes I find it rather difficult to understand what people say when they speak English.
有时候其他人讲英文时我发现很难理解。

_____

6. I miss being a child and kicking the leaves when it was autumn.
我怀念幼年时在秋天踢落叶。

_____

7. Everytime I ask someone what the best medicine is, they say it is laughter.

每次我问其他人那个药是最好的时候, 他们都会回是欢笑。

8. My parents taught me to always apologize when I have done something wrong.

我父母亲一直叫我当我做错事时要道歉。

9. Before I go to bed, I make sure to take my medicine and brush my teeth.

我上床时都会检擦我有吃完药刷完牙。

10. When I eat spicy food, my eyes tend to tear up, and people start to think that I am crying.

当我吃辣时, 我眼睛都会流泪这让他人以为我在哭。

11. My mom gave me a necklace that was given to her by her mother. I always make sure that it is hanging around my neck.
我妈妈给我一条她妈妈给她的项链。我无时无刻都把它戴在脖子上。

12. Yesterday, I was laying on my bed with my hand on my chest. I was so shocked when I could feel my own heart beating.
昨晚躺在床上时双手放在胸前。我感到很惊讶我能感觉到我的心跳。

13. When I was five years old, my dad taught me how to plant a tree.
我五岁时我爸爸教我如何种树。

14. It was only when I pricked myself that I realized roses have thorns.
当我扎到我自己时我才发掘玫瑰有刺。

15. I was taught to always make sure to water my plants, especially when the soil is dry.

我被教说要确保给我的植物浇水，特别是土壤干燥时。

Idioms

In order to really understand the roots of Chinese culture, one needs to be able to comprehend some of the most common idioms that are taught to youngsters and adults. Idioms allow us to think differently about our everyday lives, which is what the Chinese culture aims to promote. Typically, those of Chinese descent aim to be better individuals with each passing day. This is how China has become the thriving country that it is.

With the idioms below, the English translations are based off of a rough translation of the direct meaning implied by the story. Therefore, do not look too deeply into the English grammar, but instead, try to focus on the core meaning that is being portrayed.

Idiom 1

Title: A Promise Is Worth More Than a Thousand Gold Pieces/诺千金/Yī Nuò Qiān Jīn

During the Qing Dynasty, there was a man named Ji Bu. He was very straightforward, chivalrous, and loved to help people. If he was to promise something, no matter how hard the task was, he would think of a plan to complete the task, which received praises from everyone. At the time, there was a man named Cao Qiu Seng. He was a man who liked to suck up to power and wealth which made Ji Bu despise him. When Cao Qiu Seng heard that Ji Bu received a high official position, he immediately went to visit Ji Bu. When Cao Qiu Seng entered the hall, he immediately started bowing to Ji Bu and wanting to chat with him. Ji Bu did not want to take note of his presence, so Cao Qiu Seng started to flatter Ji Bu by saying, "Have you heard about a famous local saying that goes by 'receiving a thousand gold pieces is worth less than a promise from Ji Bu'? All your virtuous actions were made known by me, who has helped you spread the news everywhere." Ji Bu was immediately happy and treated him warmly. Afterward, Cao Qiu Seng carried on spreading the news, and Ji Bu's name became more famous.

Receiving a thousand gold pieces is worth less than a promise from Ji Bu. No matter how we treat people or do something, we need to keep our promises. This way we will be welcomed by others and respected.

秦朝时,有一个叫季布的人,性情耿直,侠义好助。只要是他答的事情,无论怎样难办,他都设法办到,受到大家的赞扬。当时,有一个人叫曹邱生喜欢攀权附贵,季布很看不起他。他听说季布做了大官,就去见季布。曹邱生一进厅堂,立即对着季布就是打躬,作揖,要与季布叙旧。季布不肯搭理他,曹邱生就吹捧说:"您听说过楚地的民谚'得黄金千两,不如得季布一诺'吗?您的美德广为流传。那是因为我在替你宣扬。"季布听了顿时高兴起来,热情款待他。后来,曹邱生又继续替季布到处宣扬,季布的名声也就越来越大了。

得黄金千两,不如得季布一诺。我们做人做事要信守诺言的,才会受到大家的欢迎尊敬.

Qín cháo shí, yǒu yī gè jiào Jì Bù de rén. Xìng qíng gěng zhí, xiá yì hào zhù. Zhǐ yào shi tā dá de shì qíng, wú lùn zěn yàng nán bàn, tā dōu shè fǎ bàn dào, shòu dào dà jiā de zàn yáng. Dāng shí, yǒu yī gè rén jiào Cáo Qiū Shēng xǐ huān pān quán fù guì, jì bù hěn kàn bù qǐ tā. Tā tīng shuō jì bù zuò le dà guān, jiù qù jiàn jì bù. Cáo Qiū Shēng yī jìn tīng táng, lì jí duì zhe Jì Bù jiù shì dǎ gōng, zuò yī, yào yǔ Jì Bù xù jiù. Jì Bù bù kěn dā li tā, Cáo Qiū Shēng jiù chuī pěng shuō: "Nín tīng shuō guò dàng dì de mín yàn' dé huáng jīn qiān liǎng, bù rú dé Jì Bù yī nuò ma? Nín dì měi dé guǎng wèi liú chuán. Nà shì yīn wèi wǒ zài tì nǐ xuān yáng." Jì Bù tīng le dùn shí gāo xīng qǐlái, rè qíng kuǎn dài tā. Hòu lái, Cáo Qiū Shēng yòu jì xù tì jì bù dào chù xuān yáng, Jì Bù de míng shēng yě jiù yuè lái yuè dàle.

Dé huáng jīn qiān liǎng, bù rú dé jì bù yī nuò. Wǒmen zuò rén zuò shì yào xìnshǒu nuòyán de, cái huì shòu dào dà jiā de huān yíng zūn jìng.

Idiom 2

Title: Both Lose and Are Severely Injured/ 两败俱伤/ Liǎng Bài Jù Shāng

During the Warring State Dynasty, there was an individual called Chun Yu. He was very clever and could always find many different solutions to different problems. He also had a good sense of humor.

When he heard the King of Qi state, Qi Xuan, was preparing to wage war and attack the Wei state, he immediately went to meet the king, hoping to convince him not to declare war against the Wei state. He told king Qi Xuan a story about the best hound and the most well-known and cunning rabbit. One day, when the hound was chasing the rabbit with the hope of catching him and eating him, the rabbit was running in the front with all of his might as his life depended on it. The hound was also found to be chasing behind the rabbit with all his might. The hound chased the rabbit for a long time. In the end, both of them ran out of so much energy they couldn't even move, after which both of them died of exhaustion at the bottom of the mountain. A farmer coincidently came across both the dead hound and cunning rabbit, and without needing to exert much energy, managed to carry them both home to skin and eat them.

King Qi Xuan asked Chun Yu, "I don't understand your meaning of telling me this story and what it has to do with me preparing to wage war against the Wei state." Chun Yu responded, "My king, if you were to go and wage war against the Wei state now, it is impossible to win the war in a short amount of time. In the end, both states will cause the civilians to suffer and become poverty stricken, the economy and treasury will collapse and deplete, and both sides will lose and become severely injured. And not only will the civilian's lives become unbearable, the military force will also receive a massive blow. If other states were to declare war against us now, we will have no power to defend ourselves, thus giving the other states a chance to conquer both the Qi state and Wei state." After listening to what Chun Yu said, King Qi Xuan felt there was truth behind his words, so he immediately stopped all plans to wage war against the Wei state.

If two people, whose strengths and abilities are similar, start fighting against each other, not only will they not be able to decide a winner, but both sides will also become injured.

战国的时候，有一个名叫淳于的人，他很聪明，遇见事情时总是能想出很多好办法，讲话也很幽默。

当他知道齐宣王正在准备去攻打魏国时，就去见齐宣王，想要劝说他不要去攻打魏国。他给齐宣王说了一个关于最棒的猎犬和最有名的狡兔故事。有一天，猎犬追着狡兔，想要把他捉来吃了，狡兔在前面拼命地逃，猎犬在后头拼命地追。追了很久，结果他们两个都跑得没有力气不能动弹，倒在山脚下死去了。这个时候刚好有个农夫路过，毫不费力就把他们两个一起带回家了吃掉。

齐宣王听完就问："我听不明白你说的这个故事和我现在去攻打魏国有什么关系？淳于回答 大王现在去攻打魏国，在短期内是不可能打赢的，到头来双方都会弄得百姓贫穷，钱财尽失，两败俱伤，不仅老百姓生活艰苦，兵力也会大大受到损伤，如果到时其他国趁机攻打我们，不就是让他们有一并吞掉齐国和魏国的机会了吗。"齐宣王听了淳于的话觉得很有道理，就停止了攻打魏国的计划。

如果两人实力相同互相打起来，不仅无法拼个胜负，还会造成双方受损。

Zhàn guó de shí hòu, yǒu yī gè míng jiào Chún Yú de rén, tā hěn cōng míng, yù jiàn shì qíng shí zǒng shì néng xiǎng chū hěn duō hǎo bàn fǎ, jiǎng huà yě hěn yōu mò.

Dāng tā zhī dào Qí Xuān Wáng zhèng zài zhǔn bèi qù gōng dǎ wèi guós hí, jiù qù jiàn Qí Xuān Wáng, xiǎng yào quàn shuō tā bù yào qù gōng dǎ Wèi Guó. Tā gěi qí xuān wáng shuō le yī gè guān yú zuì bàng de liè quǎn hé zuì yǒu míng de jiǎo tù gù shì. Yǒu yīt iān, liè quǎn zhuī zhe jiǎo tù, xiǎng yào bǎ tā zhuō lái chī le, jiǎo tù zài qián miàn pīn mìng de táo, lièquǎn zài hòu tou pīn mìng de zhuī. Zhuī le hěn jiǔ, jié guǒ tā men liǎng gè dōu pǎo dé méi yǒu lì qì bù néng dòng tán, dào zài shān jiǎo xià sǐ qù le. Zhèg e shí hòu gāng hǎo yǒu gè nóng fū lù guò, háo bù fèi lì jiù bǎ tā men liǎng gè yī qǐ dài huí jiā le chī diào.

Qí xuān wáng tīng wán jiù wèn: "Wǒ tīng bù míng bái nǐ shuō de zhè ge gù shì hé wǒ xià nzài qù gōng dǎ wèi guó yǒu shé me guān xì?" Chún yú huí dá: "Dà wáng xiàn zài qù gōng dǎ wèi guó, zài duǎn qí nèi shì bù kě néng dǎ yíng de, dào tóu lái shuāng fāng dū huì nòng dé bǎi xìng pín qióng, qián cái jìn shī, liǎng bài jù shāng, bù jǐn lǎo bǎi xìng shēng huó jiān kǔ, bīng lì yě huì dà dà shòu dào sǔn shāng, rú guǒ dào shí qí tā guó chèn jī gōng dǎ wǒ men, bù jiù shì ràng tā men yǒu yī bìng tūn diào Qí Guó hé wèi guó de jī huì le ma." Qí xuān wáng tīng le chún yú de huà jué dé hěn yǒu dào lǐ, jiù tíng zhǐ le gōng dǎ wèi guó de jì huà.

Rú guǒ liǎng rén shí lì xiāng tóng hù xiāng dǎ qǐ lái, bù jǐn wú fǎ pīn gè shèng fù, hái huì zào chéng shuāng fāng shòu sǔn.

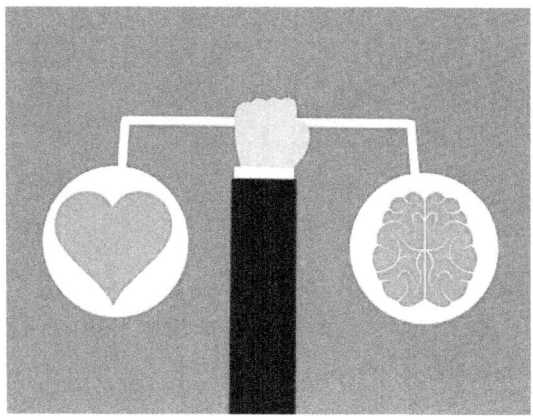

Idiom 3

Title: Fifty Steps Laughing at a Hundred Steps/ 五十步笑百步 / Wǔshí Bù Xiào Bǎi Bù

During the Warring State Dynasty, the king of Liang State, Liang Hui, asked Mencius (a wise scholar in Chinese history) why his state could not increase the population count. He said, "I have put so much thought and energy into ruling the country, and I love and protect the civilians, yet I do not see any increase in the population numbers. What is the reason behind this?" Mencius replied with an example. "During warring times, while on the battleground, it is inevitable that there will be bloodshed. If some soldiers see that their side is at a disadvantage and losing position, it is inevitable that they will drop their weapons and shields to escape the battlefield. Now, if a soldier who has escaped with fifty steps sees another soldier who has escaped a hundred steps, yet he still laughs at the hundred step soldier and chides him for being a coward, is this correct?" King Liang Hui replied, "No, they are both the same." Mencius further said, "You say you love and care for your civilians and care for their hardships, yet at the same time, you love declaring war with the other states, causing many civilians to suffer and die in war. This is the same as if a soldier who has escaped with fifty steps laughs at another soldier who has escaped a hundred steps. Both of their actions are the same. Escaping is escaping." King Liang Hui thought about this in silence, and then finally decided to end the war.

During battle, when a soldier who has escaped fifty steps laughs at another soldier who has escaped a hundred steps, it is the same as you laughing at someone who has the same faults and shortcomings as you do. The only difference is the severity. You laugh at them without even noticing and being cognizant of your own faults and shortcomings. It is the same as 'the pot calling the kettle black'.

战国时期, 梁惠王向孟子请教为什么人口不增长的原因: "我费心尽力治国, 又爱护百姓, 却不见百姓增多, 这是什么原因?", 孟子做个比喻说: "再战争的时候, 战场上相遇, 免不了要进行一场厮杀。如果有些士兵见状况不佳难免会弃甲逃离。如果一个跑五十步的士兵笑跑了一百步士兵, 骂他是贪生怕死, 这样对不对?" 梁惠王回答: "不对, 两人都一样"孟子就说："你说你爱护百姓,关心百姓的艰苦，但同时你又喜欢和其他国战争，导致不少百姓死于战争。就像刚刚比喻的战争中逃了五十步的士兵嘲笑逃了一百步的士兵,逃跑的本质是一样的。"梁惠王默默思考,最后决定要停止打仗。

作战时，逃了五十步的士兵笑逃了百步的士兵,着比喻自己跟别人有同样的缺点错误,只是严重性请一些,却毫无自知之明的去嘲笑别人。

Zhàn Guó shí qí, Liáng Huì Wáng xiàng Mèng Zǐ qǐng jiào wèi shé me rén kǒu bù zēng zhǎng de yuán yīn: "Wǒ fèi xīn jìn lì zhì guó, yòu ài hù bǎi xìng, què bù jiàn bǎi xìng zēng duō, zhè shì shén me yuán yīn ne?", Mèng Zǐ zuò gè bǐyù shuō: "Zài zhàn zhēng de shí hòu, zhàn chǎng shàng xiàng yù, miǎn bu le yào jìn xíng yī chǎng sī shā. Rú guǒ yǒu xiē shì bīng jiàn zhuàng kuàng bù jiā nán miǎn huì qì jiǎ táo lí. Rú guǒ yī gè pǎo wǔshí bù dí shì bīng xiào pǎo le yī bǎi bù shì bīng, mà tā shì tān shēng pà sǐ, zhè yàng duì bù duì?" Liáng Huì Wáng huí dá: "Bù duì, liǎng rén dōu yī yàng" Mèng Zǐ jiù shuō: "Nǐ shuō nǐ ài hù bǎi xìng, guān xīn bǎi xìng de jiān kǔ, dàn tóng shí nǐ yòu xǐ huān hé qí tā guó zhàn zhēng, dǎo zhì bù shǎo bǎi xìng sǐ yú zhàn zhēng. Jiù xiàng gāng gāng bǐyù de zhàn zhēng zhōng táo le wǔshí bù dí shì bīng cháo xiào táo le yī bǎi bù dí shì bīng, táo pǎo de běn zhí shì yī yàng de." Liáng Huì Wáng mò mò sī kǎo, zuì hòu jué dìng yào tíng zhǐ dǎzhàng.

Zuò zhàn shí, táo le wǔshí bù dí shì bīng xiào táo liǎo bǎi bù dí shì bīng, zhe bǐyù zì jǐ gēn bié rén yǒu tóng yàng de quē diǎn cuò wù, zhǐ shì yán chóng xìng qǐng yī xiē, què háo wú zì zhī zhī míng de qù cháo xiào bié rén.

Idiom 4

Title: Hearing a Hundred Times Is Not as Good as Seeing It Once/ 百闻不如一见/ Bǎi Wén Bù Rú Yī Jiàn

During the Western Han Dynasty under the rule of Emperor Xuan, the Qiang people invaded the borders of Han. They attacked the border towns and cities, conquering land, burning down everything, killing, robbing, and stealing. Emperor Xuan gathered all his subordinates to discuss and come up with a counterattack. He asked who was willing to lead the army to fight back the enemy.

A 76-year-old old general, Zhao Cong Guo, had previously been at the borders and had interactions with the Qiang people for many years. He courageously volunteered himself to take up this important task. When Emperor Xuan asked how many soldiers and horses he needed for this task, Zhao Cong Guo said, "My king, don't listen to what other people say a hundred times. It's better to go see for yourself once. It is difficult to plan and calculate how to use the soldiers properly from afar. I am willing to go there myself to see the conditions, then come up with a battle plan for the attack and defence, draw up the battle map, and then report to the emperor."

After the approval of Emperor Xuan, Zhao Cong Guo led a squadron of soldiers and set off. After the squadron crossed the Yellow River, they ran into a small army of the Qiang people. Zhao Cong Guo ordered his squadron to charge and attack. Very soon, they managed to capture a lot of captives. The morale of the soldiers was very high, and they were preparing to chase after the escaped enemies. However, Zhao Cong Guo stopped them and said, "My squadron has already traveled far to reach this place, we must not carry on the pursuit. If we were to fall into an ambush from the enemy, we will suffer greatly!"

When his subordinates heard this, they were in awe of the old general's experiences. Zhao Cong Guo observed the terrain and also found out about the plans and situations of the Qiang people's army from the mouths of the captives, understanding the enemy's strengths and deployments. He then came up with a plan to defend the borders, stabilize the border areas, and disrupt and dismantle the Qiang people's armies and plans, which he proposed to Emperor Xuan.

Very soon, the Imperial Court sent out armies to stabilize the disruptions caused by the Qiang people and secured the northwestern borders.

That is why it is always better to see and experience something for yourself than to hear it from other people multiple times.

西汉宣帝的时候，羌人侵入边界。攻城夺地，烧杀抢掠。宣帝召集群臣计议，询问谁愿领兵前去抗敌。

七十六岁的老将军赵充国，曾在边界和羌人打过几十年的交道。他自告奋勇，担当这一个重任。宣帝问他要派多少兵马，赵充国说："陛下听别人讲一百次，不如亲眼一见。在遥远的地方算计好用兵是很难的。我愿意亲自到那里去看看，然后确定攻守计划，画好作战地图，再向陛下上奏。"

经过宣帝的同意，赵充国带领一队人马出发。队伍渡过黄河，遇到羌人的小股军队。赵充国下令冲击，一下子捉到不少俘虏。兵士们准备乘胜追击，赵充国阻拦说："我军长途跋涉到此，不可远追。如果遭到敌兵伏击，就要吃大亏！"

部下听了，都很佩服老将的见识。赵充国观察了地形，又从俘虏口中得知敌人内部的情况，了解到敌军的兵力部署，然后制定出屯兵把守，整治边境，分化瓦解羌人的策略，上奏宣帝。

不久，朝廷就派兵平定了羌人的侵扰，安定了西北边疆。

所以说凡事自己看过经历过会比从旁人打听多次还有效。

Xī Hàn Xuān Dì de shí hòu, Qiāng rén qīn rù biān jiè. Gōng chéng duó de, shāo shā qiǎng lüè. Xuān Dì zhào jí qún chén jì yì, xún wèn shéi yuàn lǐng bīng qián qù kàng dí.

Qī shí liù suì de lǎo jiàng jūn Zhào Chōng Guó, céng zài biān jiè hé Qiāng rén dǎguò jǐ shí nián de jiāo dào. Tā zì gào fèn yǒng, dān dāng zhè yī gè zhòng rèn. Xuān Dì wèn tā yào pài duō shǎo bīng mǎ, Zhào Chōng Guó shuō: "Bì xià tīng bié rén jiǎng yī bǎi cì, bù rú qīn yǎn yī jiàn. Zài yáo yuǎn dì dì fāng suàn jì hǎo yòng bīng shì hěn nán de. Wǒ yuàn yì qīn zì dào nà lǐ qù kàn kàn, rán hòu què dìng gōng shǒu jì huà, huà hǎo zuò zhàn dì tú, zài xiàng bì xià shàng zòu."

Jīng guò Xuān Dì de tóng yì, Zhào Chōng Guó dài lǐng yī duì rén mǎ chū fā. Duì wǔ dù guò huáng hé, yù dào Qiāng rén de xiǎo gǔ jūn duì. Zhào Chōng Guó xià lìng chōng jí, yī xià zi zhuō dào bù shǎo fúlǔ. Bīng shì men zhǔn bèi chéng shèng zhuī jí, Zhào Chōng Guó zǔ lán shuō: "Wǒ jūn cháng tú bá shè dào cǐ, bù kě yuǎn zhuī. Rú guǒ zāo dào dí bīng fú jí, jiù yào chī dà kuī!"

Bù xià tīng le, dōu hěn pèi fú lǎo jiàng de jiàn shì. Zhào Chōng Guó guān chá le dì xíng, yòu cóng fú lǔ kǒu zhōng dé zhī dí rén nèi bù de qíng kuàng, liǎo jiě dào dí jūn de bīng lì bù shǔ, rán hòu zhì dìng chū tún bīng bǎ shǒu, zhěng zhì biān jìng, fēn huà wǎjiě Qiāng rén de cè lüè, shàng zòu Xuān Dì.

Bù jiǔ, cháo tíng jiù pài bīng píng dìng le Qiāng rén de qīn rǎo, ān dìng le xī běi bian jiāng.

Suǒ yǐ shuō fán shì zìjǐ kàn guò jīng lì guò huì bǐ cóng páng rén dǎtīng duō cì hái yǒu xiào.

Idiom 5

Title: A Word Seals the Deal/ 一言为定/ Yī yán wéi dìng

During the Warring State Dynasty, a man named Shang Yang from the Qing state wanted to change and reform the way the state was governed. When the new laws and regulations were created and confirmed, Shang Yang wanted to establish the seriousness of the new laws and regulations. He placed a log at the southern gate of the capital city and announced, " Whoever is able to carry this log all the way to the northern gate of the capital city will be rewarded with ten gold pieces." Everyone thought this action was strange, so no one dared to move the log. Later, Shang Yang raised the reward to fifty gold pieces. There was a man who was skeptical of this but still went to carry the log. He carried the log from the southern gate all the way to the northern gate. He even received the reward of fifty gold pieces. It was then that the people of the state decided that whatever Shang Yang said they would do. Afterward, Shang Yang announced the new laws and regulations.

When someone says and promises something, he/she should not then change it. It is to say that humans must be held accountable for their words and must never regret making their own decisions. People should ensure that they do not go back on the promises that they have made.

战国时，商秧想在秦国变法革新。当新的法令编制制定好了一后，商秧为了要树立新法的威信，他在首都的南门立了根木头，公布说："谁能把这根木头搬到北门，就赏给他十两金子。"大家都感到奇怪，所以没人敢动这跟木头。商秧又把赏金提高到五十两。那时有一个人将信将疑地去搬了，他把那块木头从南门搬到北门，结果真的得到了五十两赏金。人们这才相信商秧说话是算数的。商秧随后就颁布了新法令。

一句话说定了，就不再更改它。比喻一个人说话要算数，决对不能翻悔。

Zhàn Guó shí, Shāng Yāng xiǎng zài Qín Guó biàn fǎ gé xīn. Dāng xīn de fǎ lìng biān zhì zhì dìng hǎo le yī hòu, Shāng Yāng wèi le yào shù lì xīn fǎ de wēi xìn, tā zài shǒu dū de nán mén lì le gēn mù tou, gōng bù shuō: "Shéi néng bǎ zhè gēn mù tou bān dào běi mén, jiù shǎng gěi tā shí liǎng jīn zi. "Dà jiā dōu gǎn dào qí guài, suǒ yǐ méi rén gǎn dòng zhè gēn mù tou. Shāng Yāng yòu bǎ shǎng jīn tí gāo dào wǔ shí liǎng. Nà shí yǒu yī gè rén jiāng xìn jiāng yí de qù bān le, tā bǎ nà kuài mù tou cóng nán mén bān dào běi mén, jié guǒ zhēn de dé dào le wǔ shí liǎng shǎng jīn. Rén men zhè cái xiàng xìn Shāng Yāng shuō huà shì suàn shǔ de. Shāng Yāng suí hòu jiù bān bù le xīn fǎ lìng.

Yī jù huà shuō dìng le, jiù bù zài gēng gǎi tā. Bǐyù yī gè rén shuō huà yào suàn shù, jué duì bù néng fān huǐ.

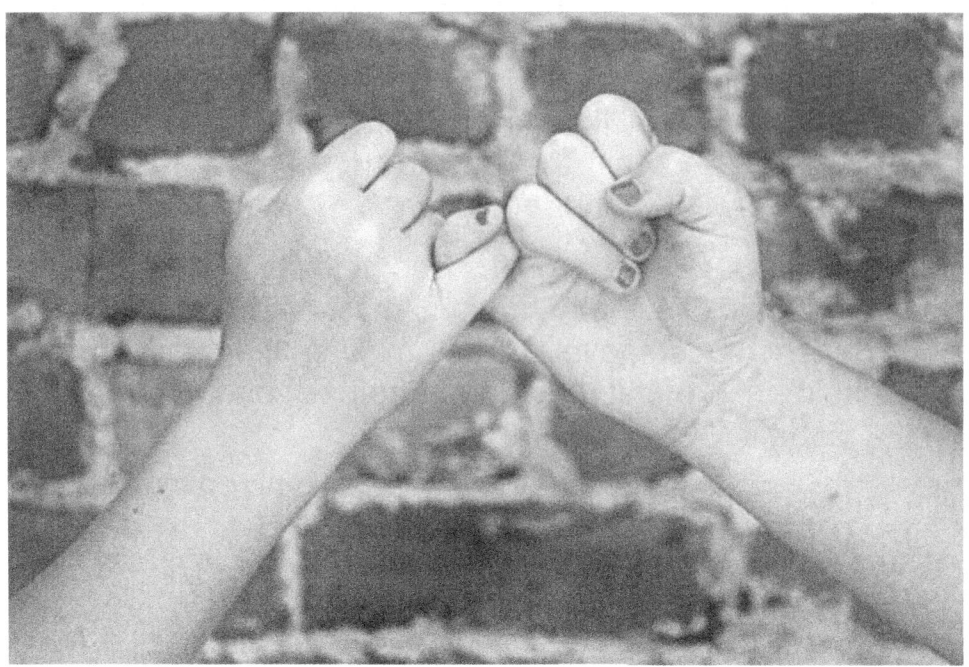

Idiom 6

Title: The Frog in the Well/ 井底之蛙/ Jǐng Dǐ Zhī Wā

There was once a frog that lived in a deserted well. One day, the frog was resting on top of the well fence, and suddenly, he saw a massive turtle coming out of the sea. He shouted to the turtle, "Hey, brother turtle, please come over. Hurry and come over!"

The frog boastfully said to the turtle, "Look, look how happy I am living here! When I am happy, I can hop around the well fence for a while; when I get tired, I can return into the well and sleep inside a hole in the brick wall of the well or quietly float around the water whilst leaving my head and mouth above water. Or take a walk in the soft mud, which is very comfortable. Furthermore, I am the owner of this well. I am free and unbound within this well. I bet you have never seen such a wide and spacious dwelling? Why don't you come to the well often to browse around?"

After listening to the frog about the well, the turtle actually wanted to take a look inside. When the turtle stuck his head out into the well to see, all he saw was a shallow well with a few puddles of water covered with moss. There was also a very pungent smell that wafted against the turtle. The turtle hurriedly took two steps back and decided to tell the frog about the sea. "Have you ever seen the sea? The sea is vast, even wider than a thousand miles; the sea is so deep, it's even deeper than thousands of feet. In the past, out of ten years, there were nine years of flooding, yet there was minimal change in the rise of the sea levels. Afterward, out of eight years, there were seven years of drought, yet there was no sign of the sea levels dropping. It is evident that the sea level is unaffected by drought or flood. Living in the sea is what true happiness is!"

After the frog heard about the sea, he was dumbfounded and at a loss for words.

有一只青蛙住在一口废井里。有一天，青蛙在井栏上休息，突然碰上了一只从海里来的大乌龟。它对着乌龟喊，"喂，乌龟兄，请过来，快过来！"

青蛙就对海龟夸口说："你看，我住在这里多快乐！有时高兴了，就在井栏边跳跃一阵；疲倦了，就回到井里，睡在砖洞边一回。或者只留出头和嘴巴，安安静静地把全身泡在水里；或者在软绵绵的泥浆里散一回步，也很舒适。而且，我是这个井里的主人，在这井里自由自在，你大概从来也没有见过这样宽敞的住所吧？你为什么不常到井里来游赏呢！"

那乌龟听了青蛙的话，倒真想进去看看。乌龟探出它的头往井里看看，只见浅浅的井底积了一摊长满绿苔的泥水，还闻到一股扑鼻的臭味。它连忙后退了两步，把大海的情形告诉青蛙说："你看过海吗？海的广大，哪止千里；海的深度，哪只千来丈。古时候，十年有九年大水，海里的水，并不涨了多少；后来，八年里有七年大旱，海里的水，也不见得浅了多少。可见大海是不受旱涝影响的。住在那样的大海里，才是真的快乐呢！"

井蛙听了海龟的一番话，吃惊地呆在那里，再没有话可说了。

Yǒu yī zhǐ qīng wā zhù zài yī kǒu fèi jǐng lǐ. Yǒu yī tiān, qīng wā zài jǐng lán shàng xiū xí, tú rán pèng shàng le yī zhǐ cóng hǎi lǐ lái de dà wū guī. Tā duì zhe wū guī hǎn," wèi, wū guī xiōng, qǐng guò lái, kuài guò lái!"

Qīng wā jiù duì hǎi guī kuā kǒu shuō: "Nǐ kàn, wǒ zhù zài zhè lǐ duō kuài lè! Yǒu shí gāo xìng le, jiù zài jǐng lán biān tiào yuè yī zhèn; pí juàn le, jiù huí dào jǐng lǐ, shuì zài zhuān dòng biān yī huí. Huò zhě zhǐ liú chū tóu hé zuǐbā, ān ān jìng jìng de bǎ quán shēn pào zài shuǐ lǐ; huò zhě zài ruǎn mián mián de ní jiāng lǐ sàn yī huí bù, yě hěn shū shì. Ér qiě, wǒ shì zhè ge jǐng lǐ de zhǔ rén, zài zhè jǐng lǐ zì yóu zì zài, nǐ dà gài cóng lái yě méi yǒu jiàn guò zhè yàng kuān chǎng de zhù suǒ ba? Nǐ wèi shé me bù cháng dào jǐng lǐ lái yóu shǎng ne!"

Nà wū guī tīng le qīng wā de huà, dào zhēn xiǎng jìn qù kàn kàn. Wū guī tàn chū tā de tóu wǎng jǐng lǐ kàn kàn, zhǐ jiàn qiǎn qiǎn de jǐng dǐ jī le yī tān zhǎng mǎn lǜ tái de ní shuǐ, hái wén dào yī gǔ pū bí de chòu wèi. Tā lián máng hòu tuì le liǎng bù, bǎ dà hǎi de qíng xíng gào sù qīngwā shuō: "Nǐ kàn guò hǎi ma? Hǎi de guǎng dà, nǎ zhǐ qiān lǐ; hǎi de shēn dù, nǎ zhǐ qiān lái zhàng. Gǔ shí hòu, shí nián yǒu jiǔ nián dà shuǐ, hǎi lǐ de shuǐ, bìng bù zhǎng le duō shǎo; hòu lái, bā nián li yǒu qī nián dà hàn, hǎi lǐ de shuǐ, yě bù jiàn dé qiǎn le duō shǎo. Kě jiàn dà hǎi shì bù shòu hàn lào yǐng xiǎng de. Zhù zài nà yàng de dà hǎi lǐ, cái shì zhēn de kuài lè ne!"

Jǐng wā tīng le hǎi guī de yī fān huà, chī jīng de dāi zài nà lǐ, zài méi yǒu huà kě shuō le.

Printed in Great Britain
by Amazon